THISTLE & THORN

BECCA LEE

431

THISTLE & THORN
WRITTEN AND ARRANGED BY **BECCA LEE**

ILLUSTRATIONS BY **BEATRIZ MUTELET**, (THOUGHTS OF SHADES)
COVER ART AND DESIGN BY
MITCH GREEN

WWW.451.PRESS

Sometimes it takes falling to pieces
to realize what we are truly made of and
to discover the strength that is hidden within.

–Becca Lee

Thistle & Thorn

Wrought Iron

I dare you to open the cage of my perfectly twisted mind, for inside you will discover how wildflowers thrive and thistles grow – how beauty flourishes and even the ordinary is made remarkable. Within these confines negativity is but a corpse buried alongside the long extinct melancholy of doubt and detestation.

So I dare you, please, to open me and promise that this cage remains without lock or key, for in my heart of hearts I know that even my greatest flaws are to someone's very own taste.

Negotiable

Find wonder and beauty
in all things, my dear,
for this world is only as ugly
as you permit it to be.

ALIVE

She was not a survivor.

Albeit she had survived, and beautifully at that, but it was her realization that there was so much more to life than simply surviving it that defined her.

Life had become about everything but survival.

For whilst all are destined for the almost forgotten certainty of death, few can say that they truly lived – that they found wonder and riches where others saw naught but sullen mediocrity.

Imbued with ardor, an inextinguishable fire burned within her. And, for the first time, 'happily ever after' was not about a perfectly told story.

No.

It was now about unraveling the hidden veracity in myth and falling in love with the delicious chaos that is life.

Flourish

True beauty thrives wherever it pleases,
it does not need permission or to be acknowledged–
that is what makes it true.

Rectitude

Speak your truths
and let your heart be heard,
for even disaster is beautiful
when it is pure.

Sacrifices

You really tried didn't you?
Tried so hard to be everything that they wanted.

I saw it.

I watched you strip and scrub yourself bare until you were left with nothing but perfectly polished bone - merely a skeleton of your former self.

Finally you were enough in your nothingness...

But I cannot help but choke on the dust that you shed- silently suffocating in the vanishing shroud of your brilliant memory.

Delicious Ambiguity

My Darling,

You must choose to grow beyond the boundaries of your despair. Seek out the light which illuminates your mind and let it shape the reality of your existence. Do not simply exist in familiar complacency, but prosper through the discomfort of uncertainty and risk. Discover your own truths in the depths of the unknown and negotiate your own wonder in this beautiful life.

Incandescent

Welcome your imperfections,
they are the soul
of what makes you human.

Starlight

Even the brightest stars
will eventually fade
into nothing
more than a brilliant memory,
but that does not stop the world
from falling in love
with their brave beauty.

Always be willing to burn
for what you love
and do not fear the end
which we are all destined to meet.
Yesterday has already passed
and we may never see tomorrow,
so let today be the day that you shine.

Hero

Darling,
your world will be
forever full of hollow heroes
until you learn to save yourself.

Essence

She was a simple girl, far too complex to define. Something that very few would know how to love.

For it would take an extraordinary soul, tainted and etched with loving scars, to truly embrace the duality of her being–

the beautiful tragedy of her tarnished innocence.

Knowledge that warmed her heart and contented her spirit. For to be loved by many is a superficial pleasure, but to be loved by just one for the true essence of her being...

Well, that was the kind of love that she would wait an eternity for.

Chipped China

You are not flawed.
You are as beautiful
as you have always been
and blessed with evidence
of a life lived.

Veteran

She was far from simple,
but she was well worth the complication.
For her smile made the days burn brighter
and her passion made the nights more potent.

She certainly did not have it all figured out,
but she knew what it was to fall hard, forgive,
and to believe in everything.

She was wild in her innocence
and glorious in her disrepair.
She lay her heart on the line time and time again
and took each break as a medal of war.

And as she sat in the recesses of her mind,
licking the wounds of her solicitude,
she knew that her lesson was not learned...

For she would never stop bleeding for all that she loved.

My Poison

If only I could bottle
the silent beat of your heart
and the essence of your soul,
so even when the coarseness of this world
leaves me parched
I could still drunkenly drown
in your everything.

More

You are so much more
than skin and bone,
flesh and blood.

You are not 'only human'.

You are human.

And that is something that no one
can take from you
as long as you remain true
to your heart and soul.

Never forget that the gift of morality
burns within you –
never lose sight of who you are.

Rebirth

And as she fell apart
her shattered pieces began to bloom –
    blossoming until she became herself,
exactly as she was meant to be.

Substance

Peel me back.

I don't want anyone to fall in love
with whatever pretty lie that they may
find above.

No.

I need someone to look beyond my flesh
and see beneath my bones, and to fall in love
with the beauty and filth of the raw mess
that they find inside.

So peel me back and see just how beautiful
my tragedy can be.

Evolution

In hate we realize who we are,
but in love we discover who we are
destined to become.

Blessed Be

Blessed are those who feel too much
and know that there is nothing ugly about breaking.
For beauty cannot exist without complexity
and we were made for this life.

The Perfect Disease pt.i

Bleed yourself beautiful,
my perfect, little butterfly.
Bleed until they no longer
call you so.

Embrace

My greatest fears melted away when you held me. For you did not hold me to keep my broken pieces together or to stop me from falling apart.

No.

You held me so that you could feel all my chips and cracks and to learn the tales of strength they had to tell. You held me without caution so that you could discover the warrior hidden within.

You

There are some people
who feel like they were put on this earth
simply to make our souls shine a little brighter
and to teach our hearts to love that little bit deeper.

Phantom

I have always admired
the gentle breeze
and the baleful wind,
for there is magnificent
and resounding beauty
in that which chooses to be felt
rather than seen.

Mantra

I'd sooner allow myself
to be crippled
by the weight of humanity
than to flourish
by the ease of apathy.

Entirety

Let someone love you in your entirety.

Let them love you exactly as you are
and for all the reasons you feared
that no one ever could –
for every mistake and every flaw.

Allow them the chance to fall in love
with both your chaos and your glory,
and know that there is greatness and beauty
in all that you are.

Let someone love you at you very best
and ugliest worst,
and experience how truly empowering
vulnerability can be.

Hidden Worth

The only tragedy of your being
is that you are worth so much more
than you will ever know...

But I suppose that is where
your true value hides –
in perfectly undeserved humility.

Unworthy

Baby, pick your battles,
and I tell you now... Walk away.

She will not be won over by your cold reflection
or sit and stroke your pretty ego.

The cage of your heart is too shallow to hold her
and she will tear your sullen kingdom to the ground
if you try to confine her heart or tame her spirit.

For she is fearless in her finity,
maddening in her majesty
and brilliant in her complexity.

Yet you underestimate her
with every malignant breath
and you will never truly know
what it is to deserve her.

Silent Sentiments

Oh Darling,
I will never understand your pain...
For you must first have a heart
for it to be able to break.

Shattered

My dear, don't you see?
You were never made
to remain unfractured or whole,
for your heart cannot bleed
its silent wonders into the world
without first breaking.

Gypsy

She was a free spirit–
blessed with a golden soul
and a gypsy heart.

Uninhibited and raw,
she wore the sun in her smile
and buried the stars in her heart.

But she was far from wild,
for she was completely at peace
within herself and the world.

Singular

Do not try to fix me,
for I am glorious in my disrepair.

Closing

Losing you will break me–
of that I have no doubt.
But the fractures will eventually mend,
for I existed before your love
and I will certainly continue on without it.
And just like old bones
that have healed through time and care,
I will feel the ache of you
on those cold and lonely nights,
but I will still rise to face the light
and bear the weight of each new dawn.
You have shaped this chapter of my life,
but your part has been played
and you do not define my existence.

Remarkable

Peace is too simple for her.
She thrives on life's poetic chaos
and lays her everything on the line
time and time again–
gathering the beautiful battle scars of life
as she falls, flourishes and persists.

You won't recognize her tomorrow,
for she has a voracious appetite
to live, learn and grow.

And one thing you need to understand is that
enough is not enough for her, nor should it be,
for she is remarkable and will not settle
for anything less from this beautiful life.

Delicate

Break often, my dear,
for it is a gift to remain
fragile and vulnerable
in this sometimes harsh,
but forever beautiful, life.

Onyx

Pretty was the poison
that led to her demise,
for when the world falls in love
with your smile
they never look beyond.

Beautiful Heart

She had this way
of always finding the good
and believing in everything,
despite all that she had seen.
And that is what I loved the most–
the pure magic of her undying hope.

Something Borrowed

She was never going to be the kind of beautiful
that belonged to someone–
a pretty doll to dress up and play the part,
be showed off, used,
and then put back on the shelf
once her purpose had been served.

No.

You could never own her.
She would test your patience,
disappear for days
and never truly be yours.
You could only sample her–
borrowing her passion here and there.

But after just one taste of all that she was,
there was simply nothing else in this world
that would do.

Putrefy

Exquisitely scathed wildflowers flourish
where the delicate decay of pretty cannot.

DRIFTWOOD

Time passes–
a desolate drift that moves like sand
through open fingers,
bringing with it the unrelenting tides of change.

The seconds breeze by and we will
weather, stumble, and slowly begin to fade.
For we were never made to withstand
the test of time.

But here I began and here I will remain–
rooted on the fragile cliff of your love.

FREE

She gave up her wings
to sate the world's greed,
yet still she looks upwards
when they can only look down.

Resides

My Darling,

Crawl out from beneath
the comfort of your skin
and lay bare yourself before me.

That empty shell is not enough for me,
for you are so much more
than beautiful could ever be.

She Was

She was beautifully human–
	broken and flawed.

So breathtakingly finite–
	both fragile and strong.

Captivatingly precious–
	bewitching and raw.

She was everything and nothing–
	she simply was.

Adoration

Hold no room in your heart
for the burden of ill will, my love.
Find the beauty in everything
for perceptions shape reality,
intent defines actions, and
forgiveness measures strength.

Fulfilled

The purpose of this glorious life
is not simply to endure it,
but to soar, stumble, and flourish
as you learn to fall in love with existence.
We were born to live, my dear,
not to merely exist.

Still Learning

I am still learning.

There are days when I forget how to love myself–
times that I give in to negativity
and allow doubt to overshadow my dreams.

I am guilty of speaking unkindly to my body,
hiding my face beneath a false mask of pretty,
and trying to change the truths of my heart.

But I can forgive myself,
and that is what makes it okay.
For I have many mistakes left to make
and I am still learning.

Finders Keepers

It was the way you so longingly and lovingly
delved into even the most shadowed chambers
of my fractured heart
that secured your place deep within its confines–
and it is there that I shall keep you,
no matter what the cost.

Heart & Soul

To worship beauty is to revere decay.
Instead, you must learn to cherish
the parts of yourself that truly matter–
the parts that will never tarnish and never fade.

Distortion

We try so hard to twist our pain
into strength, glory, and wisdom.

But sometimes, just sometimes,
pain is just painful...

And that's perfectly okay.

Spirit

It is a beautiful thing, resilience.

How even after being pillaged and abandoned,
one can thrive and come back more beautiful
than ever before.

A glorious testament
to the strength of remaining true to yourself
and never losing sight of who you are.

So fall down, break apart,
and build yourself back up–
you are simply gathering the battle scars of victory
in this beautiful disaster that we call life.

Poetic Love

If you let her,
she will love you in such a way
that she seems to hold you together
even as she rips you apart.

Virtuoso

You are the artist of your existence, my dear.
So color the canvas of your destiny
and mold the shape of your reality.
Never forget that above all else,
your life is a masterpiece of your own creating.

Blindness in Sight

The greatest wisdom
comes from those whose inabilities
allow them insight
into such things that our privileges deny us.

For we must first lack something
to appreciate the joy that it brings,
and forget something in order to remember
how it once made us feel.

So you see, my love,
to lose something is the only way that we learn
to truly cherish what still remains within our grasp.

Gardens

Pay close attention to the flowers
within your mind's garden.

Watch as they bud, bloom, and blossom,
and rejoice as their fragile beauty is born anew.

But be sure to take notice of those that wither
and know not how to flourish–
for the same conditions that nurture and nourish
some will neglect and deprive others.

Seek out those who speak to the truths of your soul
and learn to tend to both the beautiful and the wilted
with the difference and devotion that they deserve.

French Lace

She wears the
battle scars
of victory
as elegantly as lace.

Breaking Out

Never apologize for the beauty
of your existence, my dear–
negotiate your identity and be unapologetically real.

You owe no explanation for all that you are.

So do not filter your heart or plagiarize their thoughts–
scream your truths until only silence is left unheard.

Depths

Speak to me not of superficial niceties–
such discussions hold no interest for me.
Tell me of the things that set your soul ablaze
and ignite both the beauty and grim within you.
I don't believe in half measures,
so come to me in your entirety or not at all.

MISCELLANY

I know that I can find beauty
in whatever you may show me.
For even my most broken pieces
are whole enough together and,
even when I may feel like nothing,
I am still enough to be anything.

Grow

Be confident enough to be present without needing to be seen, strong enough to break when you need to fall apart and patient enough to put yourself back together the way that you were meant to be today.

And grow... Always make sure that you grow.

Passing

Our time comes. Our time goes.

Everything,
every essence and every being,
is now and forever finite.

For the recurrent cycle of time is inevitable.

So, my dear, do not fear the end.

The only tragedy of our time
is an existence bereft of life.

So live, love, and feel endlessly.

Lost & Found

The surest way to lose
your self-worth
is by trying to find it
through the eyes
of others.

Unfiltered

Unfiltered and raw,
you must learn to accept and cherish
all that you are,
and kindly forgive yourself
for what you are not.

You cannot be anything more than
your pure, perfect self–
so nurture your mind's garden,
free your exquisitely wild spirit,
nourish your old soul,
and teach your heart the power
of loving one's self.

Pulling Petals

And it took cutting back
the prettiest parts of myself
to finally realize that this shell
does not define me.
For I am so much more
than the flesh and bone
that case the beautiful tragedies
of my heart and mind.

By Her Name

The cold winter of despair
had tried its best to wilt away her beauty,
yet she blossomed still.
For her spirit was born to flourish
and she would never know the taste
of her defeat.

Landscapes

The seconds bled into hours as his mouth desperately searched her.

Consumed her.

And, at his gently calloused touch, she felt something change within the abraded interior of her once empty heart.

She relinquished her all to him and, as she watched him engulf the very essence of her being, she finally realized what it was to matter– how it felt to be enough.

Intransigence

Do not settle for an ordinary love.
Hold out for a love so extraordinary
that it makes the simple prospect
of rising to greet another day
absolutely exhilarating.

Solar

Do not be disheartened
by your surroundings, my love,
for just like the stars and moon above,
your light will shine all the brighter
for the darkness with whom it must compete.

Faith

I will always believe–
for I have witnessed hope bloom
from the darkest of places,
miracles blossom from nothing but hope,
and the beauty of dreams flourish
through the cold winter of despair.

As You Are

In the end we are who we are,
no matter how much we may appear
to have changed.

You are you.

Always have been. Always will be.

And that is why I love you –
not for what you thought you were
or what you think that you will become.

But for exactly what you are.

Nothing more. Nothing less.

Unwritten

I don't want the kind of love that they tell of in books.
The ordinary kind that can be understood–
captured and described by inanimate words.

The kind that has a beginning and an end.

No.

That will simply not do for me.

I want chaos–
a violent implosion of the very fabric of reality.

I will simply not settle for anything less.

Lengths

For you
I will learn to breathe
underwater.

UNCHARTED

When I look into your eyes,
I find a world of love staring back at me.
And I cannot help but smile
knowing that your heart is a home
that no one else has ever truly known...

One of a Kind

I will not lie to you
and tell you that you are perfect,
for not one of us is, my dear.
But you are perfectly yourself
and that is the only thing
that truly matters in this life.

Thistle & Thorn

She blooms,
even when darkness
engulfs her.

Brazen

"I am sorry..."

Three words that have slipped effortlessly
from my lips for far too long.

But no more.

I will not filter my heart
or hide my not so pretty parts–
choosing instead to wear the mistakes
of my past with pride.
For I have stumbled, fallen,
and strayed from the path,
but I am here now and as much myself
as I could ever have hoped to be.

I am beautifully blemished and unashamedly real,
and I will no longer apologize for my existence.

Scar Tissue

When you touch me, I feel it.
It lasts only a second, but for that
fleeting moment in time I feel it –
feel the weight of your world
crashing down on me.

But I do not buckle,
for the coarseness of your
scars read like braille
to the pure intent of my blind heart
and, just for a moment,
I know that I am home...

Untied

Pulling the cobwebs from beneath my skin
I broke myself, shattered,
and tied a bow around every perfect piece.
For there is unrivalled beauty
in the honesty of breaking;
a magnificence than can only be found
in the virtuous wounds of humanity.

RADIANCE

She did not belong.
I didn't know if she was born too early or too late,
I just knew that she wasn't meant for here and now.
No matter how hard she tried, she could not fit in,
    for even her darkness shone.
She was flawlessly out of place, but somehow still
more at home than anyone I have ever known.

Nature of the Beast

The only war she ever waged
was the one against herself–
the one within her heart and mind.
And what a twisted turn of fate it was
that she must first lose in order to win...
But victory, despite its defeat,
had never tasted so sweet.

Grey Matter

She stirs,
the colors of her soul blending to form
the black and white pigments
of a stark, ashen existence.

A dead world.

And just like the ocean, she breaks–
deep, dark, and doomed.

The never ending tides of her heart
pounding thick with sorrow
against the slowing eroding
rocks of my sanity.

She stirs... and I smile.

For I'd rather drown in her depths
than wade through any other water.

Mosaic

We are all a little broken, some more than others, and that's okay. Sometimes you need to break just a little to see how beautiful all the different pieces of yourself are before you put them back together in your own unique way– stronger and more lovely than ever before.

So always be comfortable and secure enough within yourself to attract attention, but desire to be felt rather than seen. Always remember that life is more about how you treat what you value than how you get what you want.

Tomorrow

Endings are never simple.

There will be times that you won't be able to see
a tomorrow without someone in your todays–
but those days will pass and tomorrow will come.
For you are not defined by anyone but yourself
and, with time, you will find that even
the sharpest pains can dull
to nothing more than a distant ache.

Trust me when I say that you will learn
to live, love and smile once again.

Ready or Not

She did not let sleep dictate her dreams.
For within her burned a fire voracious enough
to set even the brightest days ablaze.

And she was hungry–
a ravenous wolf silently stalking her prey,
eager to devour life itself.

So she bared her ambition-stained teeth
and snarled.

She was here to leave her mark on the world
and claim all that she deserved.

Autumn

Our flaws
are our most remarkable and defining features.
Each 'deficient' idiosyncrasy of our being
shapes the extraordinary individual that we are.

We all have a myriad of imperfections
and it is those less desirable nuances
that make us truly beautiful in our own right.

We all have a story to tell, knowledge to impart,
and something to learn.

Letting Go

There comes a time when you no longer care about the inconsequential aspects of life and, for me, that time is now. I no longer have the time or inclination to indulge negativity or to try and persuade others of my worth. For it's no longer about the superficial– but about substance, depth, and the meaningful. I have let go of the insignificant to allow myself the chance to care more deeply about what truly matters.

BELIEF

Her spirit thrived through her faith–
but not faith in something greater,
faith in the greatness that resided within her.

Chronicle

Here is the beautiful thing about those marks
that you don't always so proudly bare–
all those scars, wrinkles, stains, and blemishes.

They tell a story, your story,
and it is a tale of resilience
written perfectly upon your flesh.

You are one of a kind–
the only one who has lived your life
and knows your sacred truths.

So own every mark upon you,
for they are a part of the identity
that you have negotiated in this beautiful life
and you are exactly as you are meant to be.

Collaboration

You ask me why it is that I never write of you–
why I never write of the only thing that carefully holds
my fragile heart. And, with a smile, I whisper...

Because my love, I am selfish. I share my words with the world, but you... Well, you are the untold story that I keep hidden all to myself– my most perfectly prized secret. So instead, the gift I offer you is the symphony of silence– for absolutely nothing is as much of you as I am willing to share and it is the only thing that will do the unwritten masterpiece of your existence justice. So listen to the complete nothingness that surrounds us as we lie bare upon our throne of sheets and know that you are my one, my only, my everything.

Wild Heart

Do not try to make sense
of my madness
or structure my chaos.

Love me as I am or leave me be,
for this wild heart
was not born to be tamed.

Siren

If you judge her by her face
you have already missed her.
Discounted her.

She will have forgotten you
long before you blink her beauty away.

For she is unapologetically pure
and burns only with the raw intent
to show the world all that she has to offer.

If only you had looked beyond
and realized that she was so much more
than just a pretty face.

But now it is too late,
and you're just another nameless body
left in the passion of her wake.

Legacy

Bleed forgiveness with your every breath
and allow no one the privilege of planting
the seeds of hatred within you heart.

Trust me, they don't deserve that chance.

For hate is a burden that will grow within
and breed darkness until the very last spark
of your spirit has been brutally extinguished.

Allow no one that power over you–
forgive not for them, but for yourself.

Faèarytale

As the years elapsed,
her pain became her happiness,
her suffering her strength,
and her scars her wisdom.

Her passion became incorrigible
and she burned for so much more
than to merely subsist.

The echoing silence that once screamed her name
now beckoned her stay
as she began to crave existence
and yearn for nothing less than the remarkable.

She was reborn–
brutally and unapologetically.
And she no longer had need of a hero,
for she had become her own savior
in the creases of her mind–
        a heroine in her own right.

Written in Flesh

His scars tell a tale
of which he has not the
courage to speak–
a story of tragedy, love,
and forgiveness
that I will never tire of reading.

Mannequins

She did not wait for life's permission–
she made demands
and lived only on her heart's terms.

Running free,
she learned her lessons from the falls
and discovered truth
in the blood licked from wounds.

Chipped and tarnished,
she is a precious heirloom
in a plastic world.

Sweet Calamity

You look like heartbreak
wrapped up in a smile,
and I have never wanted
disaster in my life so badly.

Misfit

I promise you that I am not special, nor am I different. And, with the very same certainty, I assure you that neither am I the same. The fact of the matter is that I simply am– nothing more and nothing less. For not one of us is ordinary or put together exactly alike. There is no 'right' way for our broken pieces to fall apart and no instructions as to how best stitch ourselves back up. And sometimes, just sometimes, we need to learn to come undone in precisely the wrong places in order to find the courage and patience to start again.

So learn to negotiate your own wonder and fall in love with both beauty and disaster, for there is so much more to life than just the smiles and the wins, my dear. In fact, it could not be more about everything else. So scrape your knees and bruise your heart, and take the chance to fall just so you can get back up.

Worthy

I know it's not easy, my dear,
but you must learn to exchange
what you think you need
for that which you truly deserve.

For sometimes it takes losing
what you always thought you needed,
and surviving still,
to realize your own strength and worth.

Fruition

I know not who I am,
simply that I am forever becoming
exactly what I am meant to be.

Ebony

Walking away has never felt quite so right.
For goodbye has never come so easily
as the moment that I realized that this was
never anything more than my blind infatuation
with how a heart so black could still bleed.

ETCHED

It is easy enough
to fall in love with my smile,
the truthful happiness
that plays upon my face,
but until you learn to cherish
the scars upon my soul
and relish the darkness
that resides within my fractured heart
you will never know what it is to have me.
For there is beauty in all that I am.

ILLUMINATE

Embrace the harmony
of life's ceaseless chaos,
for our brightest hope is often
born from the darkest places.

Lessons

Some things in this world were never meant for us...
Do not belong to us.

So leave beautiful to bloom where it was born–
for it is not yours to simply take.

All that is destined for you will not wither and wilt
in your embrace.

Elysian

Naked and bound, she wore only a smile
and, with her lips, invited me to walk chosen
through the Elysian Fields of her fractured grace.
It was there that she severed my innocence
and strew it as decorative petals
across her bare body.

Unashamed in her nothing, it was in
the wake of her wild heart that I finally realized
it better to burn on as tatters
in the memory of those we have loved,
than to live forever and slowly slip
into the brittle dust of forgotten oblivion.

Sweet Acrimony

The tender murder
of your savage love leaves me
beautifully broken
and tragically complete.

EQUILIBRIUM

She said, *"...and it was when I stopped asking the unachievable of myself that I finally began to live..."*

Realizing that forever seeking to be something more only prevented her from appreciating all that she was.

It's not like she would ever stop growing,
but never again would she forget the importance
of balance and gratitude towards her becoming.

Shedding Skin

Stepping out from beneath
the skin that I've shed,
I am reborn into myself
as this old soul begins anew–
never forgetting the lessons of the past
and forever reshaping the future
as mine to take.

Slow Dance

You are at your most beautiful
when you fall apart–
breaking in perfect time
to the slow motion beat of
my shattered heart.

Come, let our pieces crumble and
our pretenses fade
so that our naked souls
may finally dance.

The Road Less Travelled

No amount of destruction or abhorrence
can purge the hating affliction of doubt.
Instead, we need venture into the obscure territories
of understanding, acceptance, and self-love.

Kintsugi

She wasn't at all put together.

She had come undone and fallen apart–
button by button, piece by piece.

But she was beautiful in all of her disaster
and strong enough to remain fragile.

For even in her fragmented grace
she was enough for herself,
and that was more than enough for me.

My Promise

Even with these long
severed hands
I promise to hold onto you
with all that I am.

Picture Perfect

"Perfect..."

The word crawled over her skin again and again – burying itself within the dirtied foundation of her heart. And, like a wild rose, it grew around her.

Climbing. Binding. Consuming.

A parasite thriving on her silent harrow
until she was left nothing but a hollow mannequin,
beautifully hidden beneath
a scarlet scream of blood and thorns.

What a perfect picture indeed...

Enough

Love is knowing all that she knows
and somehow still believing
that I am everything.

Laudable

Don't give me medicated smiles
and brittle plastic memories.
Tell me of your perfect disgrace
and let me love you exactly as you are
and for all the reasons
that you believed no one ever could.

Humility

Be humbled by the knowledge that the purpose
of life is not simply to be happy, but to feel.

You must understand that your mistakes, pain
and 'failures' are essential, and learn to
sit comfortably with them in order to conquer
that which threatens your existential peace.

Never conflate current contentment
with enduring complacency–
always strive to be the best that you can be
whilst still cherishing all that you currently are.

The Perfect Disease pt. 2

And with one last breath
the butterfly bled away
its painful beauty,
finally shedding the prison
of its perfect skin.

Her Paradox

"Who are you…?"

A question asked in rhetoric when the truth is inconceivable to those who have not experienced the truly becoming light of darkness–
to those who have not died simply just to live and who do not live for anything more than to merely exist.

So she humbly whispers,
"I am just a girl. Just a girl like all the rest…"

In the silent hope that someone will look beyond her truthful smile and dare to dance with the beautiful demons that she hides inside.

Fearless

She was fearless–
    for she knew that hell was beneath her
and the fragile gift of morality burned within her.

She was the type of girl who would find the wonder
in everything and bled beauty with her every breath.

She was together as she needed to be and broken
in all the right places–
    a fractured masterpiece of humanity.

Magnitude

Always make time for the things in life
that make your heart and soul shine.
For you were destined to flourish, my love,
not settle into mediocrity.

Inward

It was when she realized
that life wasn't meant to be perfectly fair,
that it was meant to be lived
through both the ups and the downs,
that she began to look beyond the apparent
and was finally able to see the beautiful lesson
that each moment was destined to impart.

SUBSTANTIAL

When you are true to your heart
and live with kindness,
you become something
so much more beautiful
than flesh and bone could ever be.

Corporeal Faith

There was something
in the way that she smiled
even through her tears–
she made fragile look invincible
and proved that even scars
could be beautiful.

Rise Above

In this existence of excess,
you must learn to cherish beauty
in its truest and simplest forms and
find the greatest of loves within yourself
if you wish to live for anything more
than to simply exist.

Food for the Soul

I am never going to be new.

The same storms
that weathered this rusted heart
have nourished my old soul.

So I will not shed this tarnished past,
for it has shaped me,
but it does not define me.

Goodbyes

The biggest mistake you ever made was thinking that she needed you. For she wasn't the kind of girl who needed anything but herself, and she certainly wasn't the type to chase the numbing consistency of *'once upon a time'* or the mundane simplicity of *'happily ever after'*...

She was reckless with her heart and wild in her innocence, and wanted for nothing more than to experience everything in this perfectly poetic disaster that we call life.

Aftershock

Her memory will fade, her smile will wane,
and her body will waste.

Even the soul you so desperately love
will slowly rust through the storms of life.

But don't you dare shield her from the world
or protect her from herself.

Trust her enough to blemish and survive.

For within her was the strength to move the
very mountains that once sheltered your heart.

Memories Fall

I am sorry that I could not warm the chill of ice that had set in your chest so long before we met, or that I could not free you from your mind's own prison.

I am sorry that I could not hold the sun close enough to light up your world or to make you feel like nothing was beyond your reach.

I am sorry for failing to show you how truly beautiful this life could be and just how perfect you were in my eyes.

But more than anything...

I am sorry that I simply was not enough.

Contrast

My most beautiful thoughts
come from the most
wonderfully dark places.

Metamorphosis

We have spent so much time drowning ourselves in the distraction of others that we have forgotten how to exist alone– no longer knowing how to define ourselves in the beauty of solitude. Consumed by settling into the end of our existence, we forget that life is about negotiating everything in between as we rise to meet the soaring highs and navigate the crashing lows.

So, my dear, learn how to embrace tragedy, sit peacefully with the demons that reside within you, and silence the mundane. There are so many beautifully chaotic things in this world that should never be taken for granted. You are human and you were not born to settle into existence.

Crawl out of your skin's comfort and become the greatness that is within you.

Discord

Bereft of the malady of your love,
my destitute heart beats on…
For disharmony is its own symphony.

Silhouette

Exist by the sun and
love by the moon,
for you must live in the light
to embrace the shadows
it so perfectly casts.

PURIFY

In your warm embrace
all of my yesterdays
were washed away.

Splinters

You broke me in a way that
I never thought possible.

For breaking had always seemed
such a bad thing until you tore me apart
and loved me inch by inch,
piece by beautiful piece.

Appreciation

I am grateful for every scar that I have–
for they are nothing more than a fading memory
of past wounds that have found a way to heal
and a perfect reminder
of all that I have survived in this beautiful life.

Banquet

We were made to come undone;
to be marred from the inside out
by the chaotic wonder that is life.

So give me the raw,
bloody essence of your soul–
stripped back and bare.

I want to bury myself
in the dirt of your heart
and feast on the filth
of your beautifully tragic truths.

So come undone in my arms
until your greatest fears are born anew
and your toxic complacency is put to rest.

Conviction

She did not rise above,
she grew within–
sewing her seeds of light
in the most sordid places.

For where better to bloom
her hope and beauty
than amongst the darkness
of the condemned, lost and despairing.

Diegesis

In this wonder filled world
of angels and demons,
of chaos and glory,
where there is life
there always remains hope.

For enduring morality
is the greatest gift
in the story of man–
the eminent tale of you and I.

Fortitude

She is not the girl that she used to be
nor the woman that she had thought
she would grow up to become.

She was something different entirely.

Certainly not as together as she had expected,
but somehow more complete
than she could ever have imagined.

She was softer from all the storms
and not nearly as reckless with her heart
and, finally, she was completely unapologetic
in all of her tarnished glory.

Freedom

It is when we make the choice
to let go of judgement
and seek the beauty that is within,
that we may finally understand
what it means to know contentment
within ourselves and others.

Complete

If there was one thing that she had learned
through life's trials and tribulations,
it was that her heart was big enough
to hold both sorrow and joy
and that her mind was strong enough
to allow peace and chaos to coexist.

And suddenly it all made sense.

It wasn't about wanting to be something–
it was about accepting her everything and
learning to appreciate the beauty of her complexity.

Medium

What if I showed you that everything they ever made you believe was a lie – if I told you that you are enough exactly as you are now and that you were never meant to remain unfractured or complete?

For, my dear, how would you leave a piece of yourself behind in all that you love without first breaking apart and coming undone?

So embrace your disjointed being, both tarnished and worn, for it is evidence of a remarkable and unique existence. Darling, you are a work of art– a mosaic masterpiece of your own creation.

Dear Human

Be mindful of your place in this beautiful world–
for it does not belong to you
as some might have you believe.

You are an infinitely wonderful part
of this remarkable life,
but you must learn to appreciate
and respect its smallest aspects
before you are worthy of the privileged place
that you have been granted in existence.

Do not feed the diseases of this world.
Rise above yourself,
for you are part of something so much greater.

Shards

Some think it a curse to feel too much of anything. But not I. I want to feel it all– feel the everything that this beautifully tragic life has to offer. I want to feel both love and loss as they rip through my heart, know the highs of glory and the grounding lows of shame, and fall to pieces often enough that I know exactly what I am made of before I reassemble the shards of my soul just as I want them to be.

Stardust

She dusted the sky
with the wonder of her madness,
for her mind could see beauty
that she knew needed to exist.

Pretty things

Beautiful can be many things–
and all things are capable
of being beautiful.

But beautiful can be pretty
and pretty can be oh, so
painfully ugly.

Uneven

As your lips graze
the blanket of my skin,
discolored and coarse,
you brush the sorrows
of my past clean.

Sublunary

Beauty like hers is not born.
It is suffered for, earned and shaped,
until the day that it finally becomes.
For there is nothing quite as beautiful
as the honesty of breaking
and the strength of fragility.

Treasure

...And she found riches
in the most unlikely places –
love in herself and happiness
in the poetic chaos of life.

Discussions

"I don't want unconditional love..." she said to me.

It was the first time that I really began to question everything that I had been taught about the importance of finding someone that will love you more than they love themselves. That had always been the type of love that humans seemed to yearn for.

But not her.

She did not want someone to forgive her mistakes when her lesson was not learned or someone who would breed the complacency within her. She wanted to be provoked, challenged, and stirred to be the constant greatness that was within her. She did not want someone who would allow her to slip into the mundane or fall into the routine of dying just to live and living just to die.

She simply wanted someone who could rouse her heart to be born anew with each and every sunrise–for she could not see the glory in losing herself within another.

Dulcet

She was divine
in the most devilish
of ways.

Cleanse

I know that right now you can't see it,
but I promise you that this too shall pass.

Eventually the clouds will part
and the rain will cease.

Of course, there will still be moments when pain
crashes violently against the shores of your sanity
and the cold winds of despair
will beat against the face of your weathering heart,
but you must learn to embrace them
and allow them to wash over you.

It is the storms of life that shape us.

Sweet Nothings

I will not let your compliments
dance across my ears
or your dulcet whispers
play upon my mind.

But I will let your actions
rip through my chest
and your pure intent scream
into my still beating heart.

The Beast Within

Her hair cascaded a black waterfall along the breeze; untamed and as wild as her heart. Its ebon strands licked her alabaster skin and danced about her slender frame, encapsulating her fervent presence as the wind whispered its harrowing secrets against her fractured lips.

Raw and unbound, she was breathtaking in her fragile finity.

For even when her blood stained the earth as she tore herself apart, she was still the most wildly beautiful creature that I had ever seen– glorious in her utter chaos and ready for the rebirth of her fall.

Last Supper

She knew that she wasn't for everyone.

She had rough edges where others were polished
and thorns in places that she was told
should only bear flowers.

She didn't quite fit the mold
and the cracks she had gathered through life
could break open at any time.

Loving her certainly wasn't for the faint of heart,
but it bothered her not.

For she knew that when she was for someone
it would be real and stand the test of time.

Sovereign

I am not a blank canvas.

I have been written upon time and time again– the leather parchment of my skin drenched by others' pens. Some have left me with novels and others merely with disjointed prose. You will never be the first to inject your art into me and I cannot promise that you will be the last.

I can only assure you that you will leave me embossed with an impression of your soul that will never tarnish or be rewritten.

For you may borrow my flesh, but only I have the power to bleed the final ink of my beautiful memoire.

Strip Tease

Close your eyes, my love–
for before all else you must learn to cherish
the undressed beauty of the heart and mind
that lies hidden beneath skin and bone.

Ethereal

Too often are we afraid to fall,
mistaking morality as our curse.

My dear, when will you learn
that to bleed is the greatest of gifts?

For humanity knows the bounds of life and loss
which privileges us to love as no angel,
hallowed or forsaken, may know.

So before you renounce
the discounted flesh upon you,
discover the truth
in the blood licked from your wounds.

The most vital lessons are learned in the falls
and your greatest wisdom is born
from the depths of your surmounted despair.

Your greatest strength lies in welcome imperfections.

Truthful

Do not breathe the lie
of my beautiful perfection.

No.

Save your precious breath.

Just love me in all the right ways
for all of my perfect wrongs.

SHE LOVES YOU NOT

Harrowing silence screamed her intent
as the world picked the delicate petals from her flesh.

One by one and piece by piece
they clawed at her pretty.

But even when they left her barren and bare
she smiled still...

For they could steal her pretty
but they would never know her beauty.

Sandcastles

The castles we build
to shelter our decorated bodies
are fragile and they will not last.
But the homes that we find
within the hearts of those we love
will never crumble or fall.

Silent Truths

Do not write of me as if I am something
ordinary enough to be defined–
something that can be grasped or understood.

Let the absence of me scream your love
as you grace me with the undying gift of silence.

I do not wish to be shared with the world,
nor surrender my love to one that would share me.

Selfless

Sometimes even in our everything,
our entirety,
we are not enough for some.

But, my dear, it is in the moments
that you are so much more
that you will realize your worth.

For when we are enough,
even at our bare and empty worst,
is when we may finally understand
what it truly means to be loved.

Eclipse

Have no fear, my love,
for darkness yields to the birth of new light
and you are so much more
than the shadow cast beneath you.

Run not from the truth,
nor seek refuge in lies.

Embrace what breaks you and know that
there is so much greatness within you.
You are a truly remarkable existence
and it is your time to shine.

Fertility

Breaking is just another way that we become.
For it gives us the chance
to shed light upon, and grow, in places
that we did not know existed within us.

Story Telling

She was no longer satisfied with how others told her story– finally ready for the truth of life's faèarytale.

She realized that her *'happily ever after'* was about falling in love with both chaos and beauty and finding the strength to rewrite the fate that she once believed she was passively bound by.

Sitting comfortably with the uneasiness of life's uncertainty, she relished the rapture rising within her– finally content within herself.

For the fractures had formed and the gloss of ignorance had chipped away from her skin...

And she had never felt more real.

VERACITY

Love her
but leave her brokenness.
For the truth of her becoming
is hidden beneath her scars.

Sacred Truths

Blessed am I to have seen
the delicate decay of pretty
and to have known the
undying essence of true beauty.

Corporeal

Knowing all that we cherish
in this life is only finite
makes everything
that much more beautiful
and every moment
a little more breathtaking.

Decorated

My love, do not forsake your brokenness.
I worship every wrinkle, scar, and stain upon you.
For beautiful is the evidence of life
that adorns your flesh.

Utopia

Paradise is learning to find
beauty and wonder
in even the most sordid places,
for utopia is simply the home
that we carry with us always
in our heart of hearts.

Cataclysm

There was something quite becoming
about her disaster.

The way that she could turn heartache
into something utterly beautiful with her words
and find the truest of loves within her lonesome self.

And it was in the moments that she was
enough for herself, even at her ugliest worst,
that the world did not seem quite so big –
          yet somehow still limitless.

Contusions

Do not fear the falls
and learn to cherish
the bruises upon you heart,
for you cannot journey
to enlightenment
and come out unscathed.

Dyad

I walk in life's brilliant light–
basking in the splendor of its wonder and glory.

But it is the moments that I succumb
to darkness' warm embrace
and allow her shadows to subdue my mind
that I begin to understand the true depth
of this beautiful life.

And it is in those scarce moments
of shaded revelation
that I finally know what it is to be home.

Beholder

More than anything I wish
that you could glimpse
yourself through my eyes and,
in that moment,
forget that you were ever anything
other than beautiful.

Becoming Beautiful

She buries the sorrows of the world beneath her flesh and bares the wounds of her solicitude with pride– content within the perfect knowledge that nothing can fracture what has already survived being broken.

And so I smile as I look upon her creases and cracks, for the beauty of morality burns within her. A beauty that is not born into this world, but rather one that is suffered for, earned and become– the beauty of a heart and soul so deeply scarred by compassion that all else becomes insignificant by its comparison.

Within

Not only have I made peace with all that I am,
but I have grown in places
that I never thought I would.

For within me is more potential
than I could have possibly fathomed,
a strength greater
than any obstacle I have come to face
and more heart than I thought my body could hold.

Never again will I underestimate myself
or forget to appreciate the entirety of my being.

Creation

Find the beauty in everything,
bleed kindness with every breath,
and create art out of existence.
This world is only limited by the
wonder that you choose to see in it.

Firefly

She was at her most beautiful
when she broke–
my delicate little flower
in this ever callous world.
Yet wilted and torn
she flourished still,
to become the blossom of hope
that forever guides me home.

Outlook

Live with the utmost conviction
and believe in yourself–
for the greatest love is born from within
and the greatest strength arises
from your surmounted doubt.
The only secret to this life
is learning to fall in love with everything
that it has to offer.

Fragments

Be sure to leave a little piece
of yourself behind
in every person that you dare to love
in this life.

For it is truly beautiful
how we can be carried on in the hearts
of all that we have touched,
long after the earth has
reclaimed us.

Unsound

There is no beauty
without wonder
and no wonder
without a little madness.

Journey

She hadn't always been this way– so utterly content within herself and at peace with life. It was something that she had come to be through both blood and tears.

For there was a time that simply surviving had seemed impossible – a time when she had yearned for nothing more than the smallest ray of light to break through the clouds of her mind or for a flicker of warmth to spark up within her cold heart.

But looking back on all that she had overcome, she realized that it had been the rough times that had polished her and that she was stronger for all of life's storms. She had come to understand that the only way to truly know happiness was not merely to expect it, but to work towards it by embracing contrast and learning to understand the necessity of pain.

And so her harmony came not through the complete absence of chaos, but in realizing that she was resilient enough to come back stronger from anything that she would endure.

Through these words may you realize
your perfect worth, independent of all else.
For you are a masterpiece of humanity
and worthy of this tragically beautiful life

–Becca Lee

451 PRESS
www.451.press

Lightning Source UK Ltd.
Milton Keynes UK
UKOW06f1934150416

272312UK00012B/128/P

9 781682 411957